KT-161-994

PUPPET PLAY

Goldilocks and the Three Bears

Moira Butterfield

First published in Great Britain in 1998 by Heinemann Library,
Halley Court, Jordan Hill, Oxford, OX2 8EJ,
a division of Reed Educational & Professional Publishing Ltd.
Heinemann is a registered trademark of Reed Educational & Professional Publishing Ltd.

OXFORD FLORENCE PRAGUE MADRID ATHENS
MELBOURNE AUCKLAND KUALA LUMPUR SINGAPORE TOKYO
IBADAN NAIROBI KAMPALA JOHANNESBURG GABORONE
PORTSMOUTH NH CHICAGO MEXICO CITY SAO PAULO

Editor: Alyson Jones
Designer: Joanna Hinton-Malivoire
Illustrator: Barbara Vagnozzi
Printed and bound in Italy.

02 01 00 99 98
10 9 8 7 6 5 4 3 2 1

British Library Cataloguing in Publication Data
Butterfield, Moira
  Goldilocks and the three bears. - (Puppet Play)
  1. Three bears (Tale) - Juvenile drama 2. Children's plays,
  English 3. Juvenile literature
  I. Title 822.9'14

ISBN 0 431 03481 8 (Hardback)
   0 431 03485 0 (Paperback)

You will need scissors and craft glue to make
the puppets and props for your play. Always
make sure an adult is there to help you.

CONTENTS

THE STORY OF GOLDILOCKS

Goldilocks is a naughty, nosy girl who creeps into the Three Bears' house while they are away. Now you can make some finger puppets to act out their story and discover what happens to Goldilocks.

READING THE PLAY

Four puppet characters appear in this play:

Goldilocks

A naughty, nosy little girl

The Three Bears

Daddy, Mummy and Baby Bear

Sometimes the **puppeteer** speaks. That's the person who works the puppets.

Do this part in an ordinary voice.

If you want to perform this story as a puppet show there are some tips for you on pages 6-9.

If you prefer, ignore the stage directions and read the play with a friend. Share out the parts between you.

The play is split up into parts. Next to each part there is a name so you know who should be speaking.

I'm so naughty I've crept into the bears' house while they are away. I like being nosy.

Goldilocks

Sometimes there are stage directions. They are suggestions for things you can make puppets do at a performance.

Move Goldilocks around the stage, as if she's being nosy.

MAKING PUPPETS

❧ WHAT YOU NEED ❧

* Four 10cm lengths of kitchen roll tube
* A dinner plate
* Soft fabric
* Four old socks
* Eight elastic bands
* A pencil and scissors
* Wool, card, scrap fabric
* Glue and sticky tape

1 Cut along the side of a kitchen roll tube. Roll and tape the tube around your index and middle fingers.

4 Using the dinner plate as a template, cut the fabric into a circle. Cut a smaller circle in the centre.

2 Cut the sock in two as shown. Stuff the toe end with newspaper.

5 Secure the circle of fabric around the puppet's neck with an elastic band.

3 Put the stuffed sock over the cardboard tube and secure with an elastic band. Squash it into a head shape.

To work the puppet, put your first two fingers into the neck tube. Wiggle the puppet so it appears to be talking.

THREE BEARS DECORATION

Make three bear puppets the same way as Goldilocks. Use wool for their hair and scrap material to decorate their clothes.

Cut slits through the fabric for your thumb and third finger. Poke them through to give your puppet arms.

GOLDILOCKS DECORATION

Glue on yellow wool to make long hair. Decorate the dress with scrap material. Glue on card pieces for her face.

Making Props

What you need

* Card
* Plant sticks
* A pencil and scissors
* Glue and sticky tape
* Card, fabric or paints to decorate props

Porridge bowls

Copy this shape onto card and cut it out. Paint each porridge bowl differently and tape a stick firmly to the middle of the back.

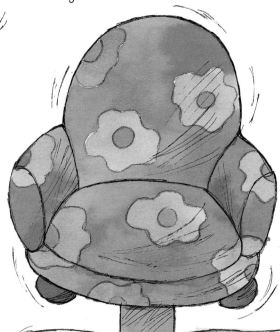

Bear chairs

Cut out three armchair shapes. The one shown on the right is Mummy Bear's chair. Daddy Bear's chair should be slightly bigger, and Baby Bear's chair a little smaller.

Decorate each chair differently. Cut a small hole in the seat of Baby Bear's chair to show it is broken. Then fix a stick to the back of each chair.

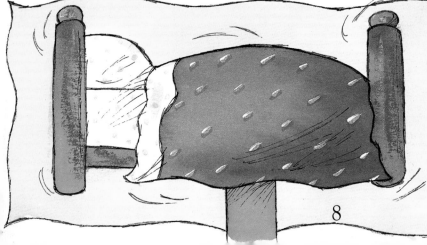

Bear beds

Cut out three bed shapes. Decorate each of them differently and tape a plant stick to the back of each one.

MAKING A THEATRE

⌐ᴑ WHAT YOU NEED ᴑ⌐

* Two bumper-sized
  cereal packets
* Two medium-sized
  cereal packets
* Coloured paper
  or paints
* Glue and tape
* Scissors

1 Cut the two bumper packets as shown. Tape back any strips that fall off and tape all the joints to make them secure.

2 Glue the two together as shown and add some tape, too, to make the join really strong. Glue and tape a medium-sized box on each side to help your theatre stand up.

3 Decorate the theatre with coloured paper or paints. Stick extra card shapes on if you like, such as a pointed top.

4 Stand the theatre on a table so you can hide comfortably behind it with your puppets and book. Prop the book inside, or lay it flat on the table. Then practise before you invite an audience to watch your play.

GOLDILOCKS AND THE THREE BEARS

Start by putting your head up and talking to the audience.

Puppeteer

Hello everyone. The star of my play has got long yellow hair and she's very naughty. Can you guess who she is?

Put your head down and put up Goldilocks, then the three bears. Say 'hello' each time in a different voice.

Goldilocks

Here I am. My name is Goldilocks.

Daddy, Mummy and Baby Bear

Hello.

Take down all the bears. Put up Mummy Bear and the porridge bowls prop.

Here we are, bears. Lovely hot porridge for breakfast.

Mummy Bear

Wiggle Mummy Bear as she eats the porridge. Make some eating noises.

Ouch, it's burnt my tongue! It's far too hot to eat yet. Let's go for a walk and let it cool down.

Mummy Bear

Take Mummy Bear off but keep the porridge bowl prop on.

Hold up Goldilocks.

Goldilocks

I'm so naughty I've crept into the bears' house while they are away. I like being nosy.

Move Goldilocks around the stage, as if she's being nosy.

Goldilocks

Hmm, let's have a look around.

Stand Goldilocks behind each porridge bowl, one by one. Start with the biggest.

Goldilocks

Yum, yum. Three bowls of porridge. I think I'll try them all.

Make eating noises.

Goldilocks

Yuk. This big bowl is too salty.
Yuk. This middle-sized bowl is too sweet.

Goldilocks: Mmmm. This little bowl is just right.

Make some more eating noises.

Goldilocks: What a shame. There's none left.

Take the porridge bowl prop away and hold up Daddy Bear's chair.

Move Goldilocks in front of the chair.

Goldilocks: I think I'll sit and let my porridge go down ... I don't like this big chair. It's not comfortable at all.

Change chairs and hold up Goldilocks in front of Mummy Bear's chair.

Goldilocks: This middle-sized chair is too lumpy. It makes me ache!

Now hold up Baby Bear's chair with Goldilocks in front so the hole is hidden.

This little chair is just right ...
Oooh, I've broken it!

Goldilocks

Move Goldilocks to show the hole.

Oh well, I think I'll go and be nosy upstairs.

Goldilocks

Take away the chair and put up the beds one-by-one. Hold up Goldilocks in front of each one. Start with Daddy Bear's bed.

I think I'll try the beds. This big one feels too hard for bouncing.

Goldilocks

Hold up Goldilocks in front of Mummy Bear's bed.

Mmm ... This middle-sized one feels too soft.

Goldilocks

Hold up Baby Bear's bed.

Goldilocks

This little bed is comfy. I think I'll take a nap.

Make yawning noises. Then take Goldilocks and the bed down out of sight.

Put up the porridge bowl prop. Then hold up one bear at a time behind each bowl. Make sure you hold each bear up behind the right sized bowl.

Daddy Bear

This porridge should be cool enough now. Hey, someone's been eating mine.

Mummy Bear

Someone's been eating mine.

Baby Bear

Someone's been eating mine and they've gobbled it all up!

Take down the bears and the bowls. Put up the chairs one by one. Hold up one bear at a time behind each chair.

Daddy Bear

Someone's been sitting in my chair.

Mummy Bear

Someone's been sitting in my chair.

Baby Bear

Someone's been sitting in my chair and they've broken it!

Take down Baby Bear and the chair. Hold up the beds one-by-one. Hold up each bear in turn behind them.

Daddy Bear

Someone's been sleeping in my bed.

Mummy Bear

Someone's been sleeping in my bed.

Hold up Goldilocks so the back of your hand faces the audience. Use your other fingers and thumb to hold the little bed behind her. Hold Baby Bear in the other hand.

Baby Bear

Someone's still sleeping in my bed. Come here quickly!

Take Baby Bear off so you have one hand free.

Oooh! Help!

Goldilocks

Use your free hand to hold Goldilocks. Make her jump up and down.

The bears are back! They'll eat me! Let me out!

Goldilocks

Move Goldilocks off the side of the stage.

Stick your head up together with Goldilocks.

Puppeteer

The bears did not eat Goldilocks and she said sorry to them.

Goldilocks

Sorry!

Put Goldilocks down and pick up Daddy Bear to shake at the audience.

Puppeteer

I hope you are never naughty or nosy. If you are, an angry bear might pay YOU a visit!

Daddy Bear

Grrr!

THE END